THOMAS JEFFERSON

PIVOTAL PRESIDENTS

PROFILES IN LEADERSHIP

THOMAS JEFFERSON

Edited by Michael Anderson

Britannica Educational Publishing

IN ASSOCIATION WITH

ROSEN

EDUCATIONAL SERVICES

Published in 2013 by Britannica Educational Publishing
(a trademark of Encyclopædia Britannica, Inc.) in association with Rosen Educational Services, LLC
29 East 21st Street, New York, NY 10010.

Distributed exclusively by Rosen Educational Services.
For a listing of additional Britannica Educational Publishing titles, call toll free (800) 237-9932.

First Edition

Britannica Educational Publishing
J.E. Luebering: Director, Core Reference Group, Encyclopædia Britannica
Adam Augustyn: Assistant Manager, Encyclopædia Britannica

Anthony L. Green: Editor, Compton's by Britannica
Michael Anderson: Senior Editor, Compton's by Britannica
Andrea R. Field: Senior Editor, Compton's by Britannica
Sherman Hollar, Senior Editor, Compton's by Britannica

Marilyn L. Barton: Senior Coordinator, Production Control
Steven Bosco: Director, Editorial Technologies
Lisa S. Braucher: Senior Producer and Data Editor
Yvette Charboneau: Senior Copy Editor
Kathy Nakamura: Manager, Media Acquisition

Rosen Educational Services
Shalini Saxena: Editor
Nelson Sá: Art Director
Cindy Reiman: Photography Manager
Amy Feinberg: Photo Researcher
Brian Garvey: Designer, Cover Design
Introduction by Shalini Saxena

Library of Congress Cataloging-in-Publication Data

Thomas Jefferson/edited by Michael Anderson.—1st ed.
p. cm.—(Pivotal presidents--profiles in leadership)
"In association with Britannica Educational Publishing, Rosen Educational Services."
Includes bibliographical references and index.
ISBN 978-1-61530-940-5 (library binding)
1. Jefferson, Thomas, 1743-1826—Juvenile literature. 2. Presidents—United States—Biography—Juvenile literature. I. Anderson, Michael, 1972–
E332.79.T56 2012
973.4'6092—dc23
[B]

2012015598

Manufactured in the United States of America

On the cover, p. 3 (background image): Jefferson, along with other members of the committee that drafted the Declaration of Independence, presenting the document to the Continental Congress in 1776. *Universal Images Group/Getty Images*

Cover, page 3 (portrait): Universal Images Group/Getty Images; cover, pp. 1, 3 (flag) © iStockphoto.com/spxChrome; pp. 5, 12, 25, 39, 47, 61, 71, 74, 77, 79 Fedorov Oleksiy/Shutterstock.com

Table of Contents

Introduction

Although Thomas Jefferson held many titles over the course of his life—secretary of state, vice president, and president the most prominent among them—the title of "architect" may have suited him best. Not only did he design buildings (his own home being one notable example), but as primary author of the Declaration of Independence, cofounder of the Republican party, and engineer of the Louisiana Purchase, he also helped craft a nation. Indeed, the foundation of the United States rests on many of the contributions Jefferson made to law and governance. The remarkable life of this Founding Father is chronicled in the following pages.

Jefferson's passions were many and his accomplishments widespread. From a young age, he developed and indulged interests as diverse as music, classical literature, science, and architecture, ultimately choosing to pursue a legal career. First cast into the public eye as a representative in Virginia's House of Burgesses, Jefferson began to demonstrate his talent for public service during the trying period of the American Revolution. He was appointed as Virginia's delegate to the Second Continental Congress, a body of representatives assembled to assess the colonies' best interests. There Jefferson, alongside such other luminaries as Benjamin Franklin and John Adams, penned the Declaration of Independence, which announced the colonies' reasons for separation from Britain. The document, written primarily by Jefferson, would become a symbol of national pride and liberty both in the United States and around the world.

Following his retirement from the Continental Congress, Jefferson would go on to hold a variety of political posts at the state and national levels. He first returned to the Virginia legislature, where he helped set several important precedents, including the separation of church and state, in the Virginia constitution. After serving as governor of Virginia for one term, Jefferson returned to the Continental Congress, bringing with him ideas about liberty and equality that he had championed as a legislator. He went on to serve as U.S. ambassador to France, returning to the United States to serve as secretary of state under the first U.S. president, George Washington.

It was during Jefferson's time as secretary of state that his political views crystallized

The Jefferson Memorial in Washington, D.C., at dusk. The memorial was dedicated on April 13, 1943, the 200th aniversary of Jefferson's birth. Lester Lefkowitz/The Image Bank/Getty Images

with the foundation of the Republican party. He believed in states' rights, a limited role for the central government, and a strict interpretation of the Constitution. This pitted him against the Federalists—led by Alexander Hamilton and John Adams—who controlled Washington's administration and resulted in Jefferson's resignation as secretary. He re-emerged on the national stage in 1796 when he decided to run for president. However, Jefferson lost to Adams and became vice president.

Jefferson made a second run for the presidency in 1800 and this time met with success. Amongst a host of domestic and foreign challenges, Jefferson orchestrated perhaps the greatest achievement of his tenure—the Louisiana Purchase. To Jefferson the land west of the Mississippi River represented new opportunities and resources for the United States. When France decided to sell its territory between the Mississippi and the Rocky Mountains, Jefferson took advantage of the situation. Despite his reservations about the constitutionality of such a purchase, Jefferson forged ahead with negotiations and purchased all the land for 15 million dollars, thereby doubling the area of the United States. He served another term as president before retiring in 1809.

Even as he established himself as a public figure, Jefferson reserved room for his personal interests and private life. In 1768 he designed a mansion near Shadwell, Va., which he called Monticello and maintained until his death. He lived there with his wife, Martha, and their children Patsy and Polly. He pursued his love of architecture throughout his life, designing the Virginia Capitol during his time as ambassador to France and the University of Virginia after his retirement.

Despite the clarity of thought and vision attributed to Jefferson, he was not without his weaknesses. For example, his position on slavery appeared inconsistent and malleable over the course of his life. Although Jefferson was a slave owner himself, he initially advocated ending the slave trade. Later, however, he distanced himself from the antislavery movement, even supporting the expansion of slavery into new territories.

Following the death of his wife, Jefferson's personal life also became the subject of some controversy. While in France, Jefferson pursued an intimate relationship with a married woman. Later, allegations surfaced of Jefferson's affair with Sally Hemings, one of his slaves, and it is believed that Jefferson fathered at least one of her children. While there is still some uncertainty surrounding the details of the relationship, there is evidence of a genetic link between Jefferson and at least some of Hemings' offspring.

A consummate scholar and statesman, Jefferson was a steady presence in a rapidly changing political and cultural environment, and even his missteps cannot diminish his significance to history. With a voice immortalized in the Declaration of Independence and a legacy that included expanding the size and stature of the United States, Jefferson was invaluable in shaping the character of the nation.

CHAPTER 1

Early Life and Political Career

An agent of the American Revolution and the author of the Declaration of Independence in 1776, Thomas Jefferson was an active statesman who from 1801 to 1809 served as the third president of the United States. During his presidency the territory of the United States doubled with the Louisiana Purchase. To investigate the vastness of this newly acquired land in the West, he dispatched two of the most famous explorers in U.S. history, Meriwether Lewis and William Clark, to blaze a trail through the Rocky Mountains to the Pacific Ocean. In the first overseas war in U.S. history Jefferson sent military forces to the Mediterranean Sea to crush Tripoli's piracy threats.

Thomas Jefferson. SuperStock/Getty Images

Jefferson entered the political arena in 1769 as a Virginia state legislator. From 1775 to 1801 he held several notable public positions, including Continental Congress delegate, governor of Virginia, U.S. secretary of state, and vice president of the United States. His time in Paris during the 1780s as U.S. ambassador to France brought about more controversy concerning his personal life than any achievements in foreign relations. An alleged love affair with Sally Hemings, one of his slaves whom he summoned to Paris, sparked a paternity debate that persisted long after his death.

Jefferson initiated free public education and the separation of church and state in Virginia, which were the cornerstones for these reforms throughout the nation. As an activist for states' rights, Jefferson founded the Republican party to contend with Federalist ideals of a powerful federal government. A Founding Father of his country, Jefferson inspired a sense of nationalistic pride for the United States based on liberty and human rights.

FAMILY AND EDUCATION

Thomas Jefferson was born on April 13 (April 2 according to the calendar used then), 1743, in Shadwell, Va. His parents were Peter Jefferson and Jane Randolph Jefferson. Peter Jefferson was a landowner, surveyor, and public official of Albemarle County. Jane Randolph Jefferson was descended from one of the most prominent families in Virginia. The couple had two sons, of whom Thomas was the eldest, and six daughters.

In 1745 Peter Jefferson moved his family to Tuckahoe, the Randolph plantation

The garden at Tuckahoe Plantation near Richmond, Va., where Jefferson spent part of his childhood. © AP Images

near Richmond, Va. Thomas was educated by private tutors until 1752, when his family returned to Shadwell. He continued his education at two boarding schools in Virginia, first in Northam and later in Fredericksville, until age 16.

As a child Thomas enjoyed learning and developed a love of the arts. His musical interests included dancing, singing, and playing the violin. He read classical literature and mastered Greek and Latin. He also spent his time outdoors exploring and studying nature around the foothills of the Blue Ridge Mountains near Shadwell. He excelled in science and architecture and was devoted to achieving a well-rounded education.

Peter Jefferson died in 1757, and Thomas became proprietor of the family estate because the law of primogeniture in Virginia granted the eldest son in a family the exclusive right to the father's inheritance. Jane Jefferson died in 1776, but little else is known about her life between 1757 and 1776 because Thomas made little mention of her in his memoirs.

Thomas Jefferson enrolled at the College of William and Mary in Williamsburg, Va., in 1760. In his first two years he studied mathematics and science under William Small and history and law under George Wythe, one of the leading scholars in Virginia. Jefferson applied himself vigorously to his lessons, often spending up to 15 hours a day studying. He pursued a career in law under Wythe's guidance beginning in 1762. He gained admittance to the Virginia bar in April 1767 and earned a reputation as a distinguished legal scholar.

One of the major architectural projects that Jefferson took on during his life was the design and construction of his own home, Monticello, located near his birthplace of Shadwell, Va.

Jefferson returned to Shadwell in 1768 and applied his architectural skills to build a mansion on an 867-foot (264-meter) mountain nearby. He named his new estate Monticello, an Italian word meaning "little mountain."

On Jan. 1, 1772, Jefferson married Martha Wayles Skelton, a widow. Her estate more than doubled Jefferson's landholdings when the couple combined their properties.

DECLARATION OF INDEPENDENCE

In 1769 Jefferson was elected to the House of Burgesses, Virginia's representative assembly, in Williamsburg. He employed his comprehensive knowledge of law to support the colonial opposition to British legislation and taxation. He emphasized that Great Britain had no legal authority to govern and delegate authority in the colonies.

Jefferson's first published essay, "A Summary View of the Rights of British America" (1774), insisted upon independence from Great Britain as the only solution to liberate the oppressed colonies. After his essay was published, most of the Virginia legislature was not prepared to accept such a radical

Martha Jefferson

Thomas Jefferson's wife, Martha Wayles Skelton Jefferson, was never a first lady. She died 19 years before her husband was sworn into office in 1801.

Martha Wayles was born on Oct. 30 (Oct. 19 on the calendar used then), 1748, at her family's plantation home in Charles City County, Va. She married Bathurst Skelton in 1766, but he died two years later. The young widow returned to her parents' house with her young son, John, who later died at the age of 3. She married Thomas Jefferson on Jan. 1, 1772, and they soon moved to his home, Monticello. Music often filled their house, with him playing the violin and her, the pianoforte.

The Jeffersons had six children, but only Martha (called Patsy, born in 1772) and Maria (baptized Mary but called Polly, born in 1778) survived past early childhood. Two daughters

Martha Jefferson. After her passing, Jefferson destroyed their correspondence, and this silhouette is the only known image of her. **MPI/Archive Photos/Getty Images**

and a son died in infancy, and their last child, Lucy, died of whooping cough at age 2. Martha was weakened by the physical strain of so many pregnancies. Thomas, wanting to stay near his sickly wife, would not accept an appointment by the Continental Congress as a commissioner to France but did serve in Virginia's House of Delegates and as governor.

Martha died on Sept. 6, 1782, at Monticello. Although the exact cause of her death is unknown, documents indicate that she never recovered after Lucy's birth in May 1782. Jefferson went into seclusion for weeks following his wife's death, and later in the year he accepted the post he had earlier declined in France. Wanting to keep his memories of Martha private, he burned all their letters to one another and did not speak of her much after her death.

After Jefferson became president, he often called upon Dolley Madison, wife of his secretary of state, James Madison, to handle social events at the White House. On other occasions, his daughters Patsy and Polly served as hostesses. During Jefferson's second administration, Patsy gave birth to a son, the first baby ever to be born in the White House.

position against Great Britain. However, over the next year hostilities between the colonists and British authorities reached a boiling point, and the American Revolution began in Massachusetts at the Battles of Lexington and Concord in 1775.

In that same year the Virginia legislature appointed Jefferson as a delegate to the Second Continental Congress in Philadelphia. The Continental Congress recognized his idea

Minutemen confronting British troops during the Battle of Lexington in 1775, the first skirmish of the American Revolution. **Hulton Archive/Getty Images**

***Benjamin Franklin* (left), *John Adams* (center), *and Jefferson, working on a draft of the Declaration of Independence.* Universal Images Group/Getty Images**

for the colonies to secede from British rule as the best course of action.

On June 11, 1776, Jefferson was selected to a committee, which included John Adams and Benjamin Franklin, to outline a formal document justifying the reasons for declaring independence from Great Britain. The committee members admired Jefferson's talent for influential writing and chose him to prepare the first draft. His words expressed what a majority of colonial citizens desired when he wrote: "We hold these truths to be self-evident, that all men are created equal, that they are endowed by their Creator with

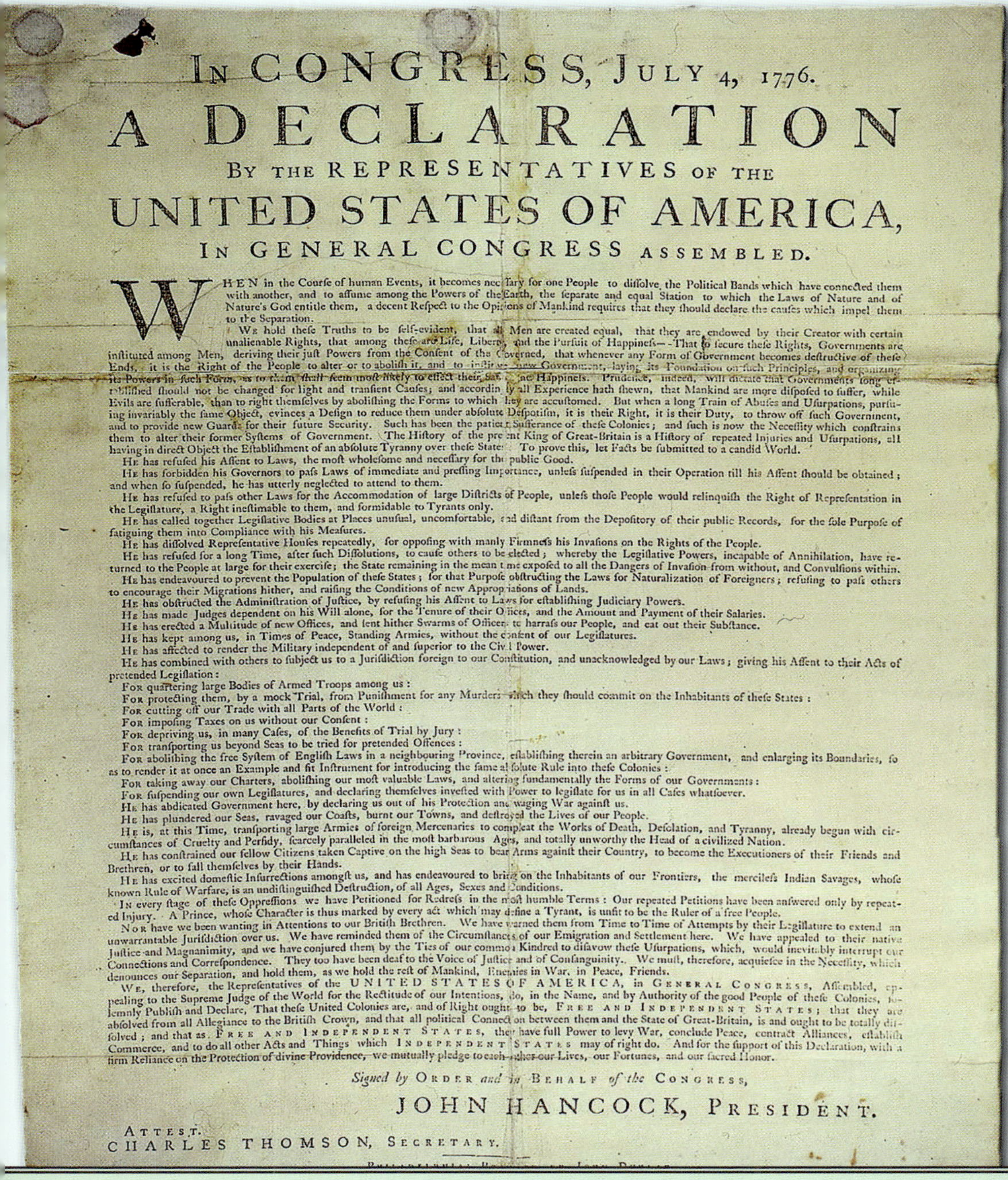

IN CONGRESS, JULY 4, 1776.

A DECLARATION

BY THE REPRESENTATIVES OF THE

UNITED STATES OF AMERICA,

IN GENERAL CONGRESS ASSEMBLED.

WHEN in the Course of human Events, it becomes necessary for one People to dissolve the Political Bands which have connected them with another, and to assume among the Powers of the Earth, the separate and equal Station to which the Laws of Nature and of Nature's God entitle them, a decent Respect to the Opinions of Mankind requires that they should declare the causes which impel them to the Separation.

WE hold these Truths to be self-evident, that all Men are created equal, that they are endowed by their Creator with certain unalienable Rights, that among these are Life, Liberty, and the Pursuit of Happiness—That to secure these Rights, Governments are instituted among Men, deriving their just Powers from the Consent of the Governed, that whenever any Form of Government becomes destructive of these Ends, it is the Right of the People to alter or to abolish it, and to institute new Government, laying its Foundation on such Principles, and organizing its Powers in such Form, as to them shall seem most likely to effect their Safety and Happiness. Prudence, indeed, will dictate that Governments long established should not be changed for light and transient Causes; and accordingly all Experience hath shewn, that Mankind are more disposed to suffer, while Evils are sufferable, than to right themselves by abolishing the Forms to which they are accustomed. But when a long Train of Abuses and Usurpations, pursuing invariably the same Object, evinces a Design to reduce them under absolute Despotism, it is their Right, it is their Duty, to throw off such Government, and to provide new Guards for their future Security. Such has been the patient Sufferance of these Colonies; and such is now the Necessity which constrains them to alter their former Systems of Government. The History of the present King of Great-Britain is a History of repeated Injuries and Usurpations, all having in direct Object the Establishment of an absolute Tyranny over these States. To prove this, let Facts be submitted to a candid World.

HE has refused his Assent to Laws, the most wholesome and necessary for the public Good.

HE has forbidden his Governors to pass Laws of immediate and pressing Importance, unless suspended in their Operation till his Assent should be obtained; and when so suspended, he has utterly neglected to attend to them.

HE has refused to pass other Laws for the Accommodation of large Districts of People, unless those People would relinquish the Right of Representation in the Legislature, a Right inestimable to them, and formidable to Tyrants only.

HE has called together Legislative Bodies at Places unusual, uncomfortable, and distant from the Depository of their public Records, for the sole Purpose of fatiguing them into Compliance with his Measures.

HE has dissolved Representative Houses repeatedly, for opposing with manly Firmness his Invasions on the Rights of the People.

HE has refused for a long Time, after such Dissolutions, to cause others to be elected; whereby the Legislative Powers, incapable of Annihilation, have returned to the People at large for their exercise; the State remaining in the mean time exposed to all the Dangers of Invasion from without, and Convulsions within.

HE has endeavoured to prevent the Population of these States; for that Purpose obstructing the Laws for Naturalization of Foreigners; refusing to pass others to encourage their Migrations hither, and raising the Conditions of new Appropriations of Lands.

HE has obstructed the Administration of Justice, by refusing his Assent to Laws for establishing Judiciary Powers.

HE has made Judges dependent on his Will alone, for the Tenure of their Offices, and the Amount and Payment of their Salaries.

HE has erected a Multitude of new Offices, and sent hither Swarms of Officers to harrass our People, and eat out their Substance.

HE has kept among us, in Times of Peace, Standing Armies, without the consent of our Legislatures.

HE has affected to render the Military independent of and superior to the Civil Power.

HE has combined with others to subject us to a Jurisdiction foreign to our Constitution, and unacknowledged by our Laws; giving his Assent to their Acts of pretended Legislation:

FOR quartering large Bodies of Armed Troops among us:

FOR protecting them, by a mock Trial, from Punishment for any Murders which they should commit on the Inhabitants of these States:

FOR cutting off our Trade with all Parts of the World:

FOR imposing Taxes on us without our Consent:

FOR depriving us, in many Cases, of the Benefits of Trial by Jury:

FOR transporting us beyond Seas to be tried for pretended Offences:

FOR abolishing the free System of English Laws in a neighbouring Province, establishing therein an arbitrary Government, and enlarging its Boundaries, so as to render it at once an Example and fit Instrument for introducing the same absolute Rule into these Colonies:

FOR taking away our Charters, abolishing our most valuable Laws, and altering fundamentally the Forms of our Governments:

FOR suspending our own Legislatures, and declaring themselves invested with Power to legislate for us in all Cases whatsoever.

HE has abdicated Government here, by declaring us out of his Protection and waging War against us.

HE has plundered our Seas, ravaged our Coasts, burnt our Towns, and destroyed the Lives of our People.

HE is, at this Time, transporting large Armies of foreign Mercenaries to compleat the Works of Death, Desolation, and Tyranny, already begun with circumstances of Cruelty and Perfidy, scarcely paralleled in the most barbarous Ages, and totally unworthy the Head of a civilized Nation.

HE has constrained our fellow Citizens taken Captive on the high Seas to bear Arms against their Country, to become the Executioners of their Friends and Brethren, or to fall themselves by their Hands.

HE has excited domestic Insurrections amongst us, and has endeavoured to bring on the Inhabitants of our Frontiers, the merciless Indian Savages, whose known Rule of Warfare, is an undistinguished Destruction, of all Ages, Sexes and Conditions.

IN every stage of these Oppressions we have Petitioned for Redress in the most humble Terms: Our repeated Petitions have been answered only by repeated Injury. A Prince, whose Character is thus marked by every act which may define a Tyrant, is unfit to be the Ruler of a free People.

NOR have we been wanting in Attentions to our British Brethren. We have warned them from Time to Time of Attempts by their Legislature to extend an unwarrantable Jurisdiction over us. We have reminded them of the Circumstances of our Emigration and Settlement here. We have appealed to their native Justice and Magnanimity, and we have conjured them by the Ties of our common Kindred to disavow these Usurpations, which, would inevitably interrupt our Connections and Correspondence. They too have been deaf to the Voice of Justice and of Consanguinity. We must, therefore, acquiesce in the Necessity, which denounces our Separation, and hold them, as we hold the rest of Mankind, Enemies in War, in Peace, Friends.

WE, therefore, the Representatives of the UNITED STATES OF AMERICA, in GENERAL CONGRESS, Assembled, appealing to the Supreme Judge of the World for the Rectitude of our Intentions, do, in the Name, and by Authority of the good People of these Colonies, solemnly Publish and Declare, That these United Colonies are, and of Right ought to be, FREE AND INDEPENDENT STATES; that they are absolved from all Allegiance to the British Crown, and that all political Connection between them and the State of Great-Britain, is and ought to be totally dissolved; and that as FREE AND INDEPENDENT STATES, they have full Power to levy War, conclude Peace, contract Alliances, establish Commerce, and to do all other Acts and Things which INDEPENDENT STATES may of right do. And for the support of this Declaration, with a firm Reliance on the Protection of divine Providence, we mutually pledge to each other our Lives, our Fortunes, and our sacred Honor.

Signed by ORDER *and in* BEHALF *of the* CONGRESS,

JOHN HANCOCK, PRESIDENT.

ATTEST.
CHARLES THOMSON, SECRETARY.

he Declaration of Independence. U.S. National Archives and Records Administration

certain unalienable Rights, that among these are Life, Liberty, and the pursuit of Happiness...."

The Continental Congress adopted the Declaration of Independence on July 4, 1776, which officially announced the separation of the 13 colonies from Great Britain. Jefferson and other delegates signed it, but he was not credited as the principal author until 1790. Between 1776 and 1777 the Continental Congress wrote the Articles of Confederation, which was ratified in 1781 as the first constitution of the United States

CHAPTER 2

State and National Offices

Jefferson retired from the Continental Congress in October 1776 and returned to serve in the Virginia legislature. In the next few years he worked to reform the state's legal code to bring it in line with the principles of the American Revolution. He then served as governor of Virginia before returning to national politics, first as a Continental Congress delegate and then as U.S. ambassador to France.

Virginia Legislator and Governor

With the assistance of his colleague James Madison, Jefferson drafted the Virginia constitution complete with a declaration of

James Madison. Hulton Archive/Getty Images

rights. The two delegates proposed statutory reforms in Virginia that eventually set a standard for the entire nation. Jefferson secured the abolishment of primogeniture. He also presented amendments to establish an expense-free public school system for all citizens of Virginia and lobbied for state support of higher education. The Virginia constitution served as a model for the United States Constitution.

In 1777 Jefferson wrote the Virginia Statute for Religious Freedom, which provided for the complete separation of church and state. After nine years of deliberation and the skillful persuasive tactics of Madison, his primary supporter, the Virginia legislature enacted the statute in 1786. Under this law, the state of Virginia was required to tolerate all religions without preference to any particular denomination. People of Virginia were allowed to follow their own religious beliefs without political discrimination. Jefferson's proposals reflected his vision of creating a government that served and protected the rights of citizens.

Jefferson was elected governor of Virginia in 1779. The office allowed him very little authority and no veto power because the governor's cabinet, called the Council of State, delegated the state's laws and advised him on all administrative tasks. His most significant accomplishment as governor was having the state capital relocated from Williamsburg to Richmond in 1780.

The American Revolution reached Virginia in 1780 as British troops invaded Richmond. Jefferson's administration retreated from the capital and established a temporary base in Charlottesville, while he assembled his family at Monticello. The Virginia press labeled him a coward for abandoning his duties as governor. In 1781 he retired from public life after his term as governor and returned to his home at Monticello.

Return to the Continental Congress

Martha Jefferson died in September 1782, leaving Thomas to raise their two daughters, Patsy and Polly. He was devastated from the loss of his beloved wife and vowed never to marry again. His retirement was short-lived, however, as he agreed to serve as a Virginia delegate to the Continental Congress in December 1782.

Jefferson petitioned for laws in the Continental Congress with the same values of freedom and equality that he upheld in the Virginia legislature. The American Revolution ended with the Treaty of Paris in 1783, and the western boundary of the United States was established at the Mississippi River. Jefferson requested that the Continental Congress allow the territories west of the Mississippi to apply for

From left to right, John Adams, Robert Morris, Alexander Hamilton, and Jefferson, all delegates to the Continental Congress. Library of Congress Prints and Photographs Division

statehood after they met certain population and organizational standards. He also sought to abolish slavery in any newly acquired U.S. territories and to free all slaves in the United States born after 1800. Both proposals, which may have changed the course of U.S. history, were defeated by a narrow margin in the Continental Congress.

YEARS IN PARIS

The Continental Congress sent Jefferson to Paris in 1784 to succeed Benjamin Franklin as U.S. ambassador to France. Jefferson joined John Adams in negotiating with European nations for open international trade markets. Jefferson and Adams also acquired a loan from the Netherlands that allowed the United States to consolidate its foreign debts. While in Paris, the two diplomats formed a personal friendship that would later transform into a bitter political rivalry.

Jefferson also attempted to ally European countries with the United States against North Africa's Barbary pirates who were attacking merchant vessels in the Mediterranean Sea. Despite his efforts, Jefferson was unable to secure any trade agreements or strong

The Maison-Carrée, an ancient Roman temple in Nîmes, France. The building inspired Jefferson's design for the Virginia Capitol. JNS/Gamma-Rapho/Getty Images

European alliances for the United States during his four years in Paris.

During his spare time in Paris, Jefferson indulged in the abundance of French arts

Maria Cosway. © Huntington Library/SuperStock

and entertainment. He toured museums and gardens, attended theatrical performances and operas, and consumed the finest French cuisine and wine. He was fond of the architecture in France and designed the new Virginia Capitol, which was built in 1785, by modeling it on the Maison-Carrée (Squared House) in Nîmes, France.

Jefferson's attendance at art exhibits in Paris led to his acquaintance with Maria Cosway. Maria was married to Richard Cosway, an English miniaturist, or painter of small portraits. Jefferson and Maria Cosway shared similar interests as they visited art shows and galleries together in Paris. When the Cosways left Paris in 1787, Jefferson exchanged letters with Maria in which he expressed his deep affection for her. He either lost heart or thought better about their relationship and eventually ended their correspondence. Afterward he turned his attention back to business in Paris.

Jefferson's daughter Patsy accompanied him to Paris in 1784, and he sent for Polly in 1787 to join them. Once his daughters were with him in Paris, he placed both girls in a convent to shelter them from the prevalent temptations of greed, drunkenness, and lust in society.

Jefferson's elder daughter, Martha (Patsy). Three Lions/Hulton Archive/Getty Images

Jefferson and Sally Hemings

The most controversial segment of Jefferson's personal life was his alleged love affair with his mulatto slave, Sally Hemings. Historians speculated that the affair began after Hemings arrived in Paris with Polly Jefferson in 1787. Scholars estimated that he fathered at least one and possibly six of Hemings' children. Research continued, and in 1998 scientists conducted a DNA analysis on some of Jefferson's and Hemings' living descendants. The tests showed that it was almost certain that Jefferson and Hemings had children together. Nevertheless, their relationship remains a topic of debate.

Jefferson's descendants and those of Sally Hemings posing together at Jefferson's plantation during a reunion in 1999. DNA evidence suggests that at least some of Hemings' children were fathered by Jefferson. © AP Images

The Issue of Slavery

Jefferson's position on slavery was complex. In the 1760s and '70s he and his fellow Virginia planters, all of whom owned slaves, supported the end of the slave trade in the colonies. In his only book, *Notes on the State of Virginia* (1781), Jefferson discussed how slavery violated human rights and contradicted the principles of freedom and equality upon which the United States was founded. His proposals in the Continental Congress during the 1780s were aimed at gradually abolishing slavery, starting with new U.S. territories and newborn slaves. These statements and actions put Jefferson at the forefront of the antislavery movement.

By the time he returned to the United States in 1789, however, Jefferson had backed away from a leadership role against slavery. His position had generated controversy, especially within the planter class of Virginia, that Jefferson wanted to avoid. In addition, it was clear that Jefferson's position was inconsistent. Alongside his antislavery arguments in *Notes on the State of Virginia*, he also asserted that people of African descent were

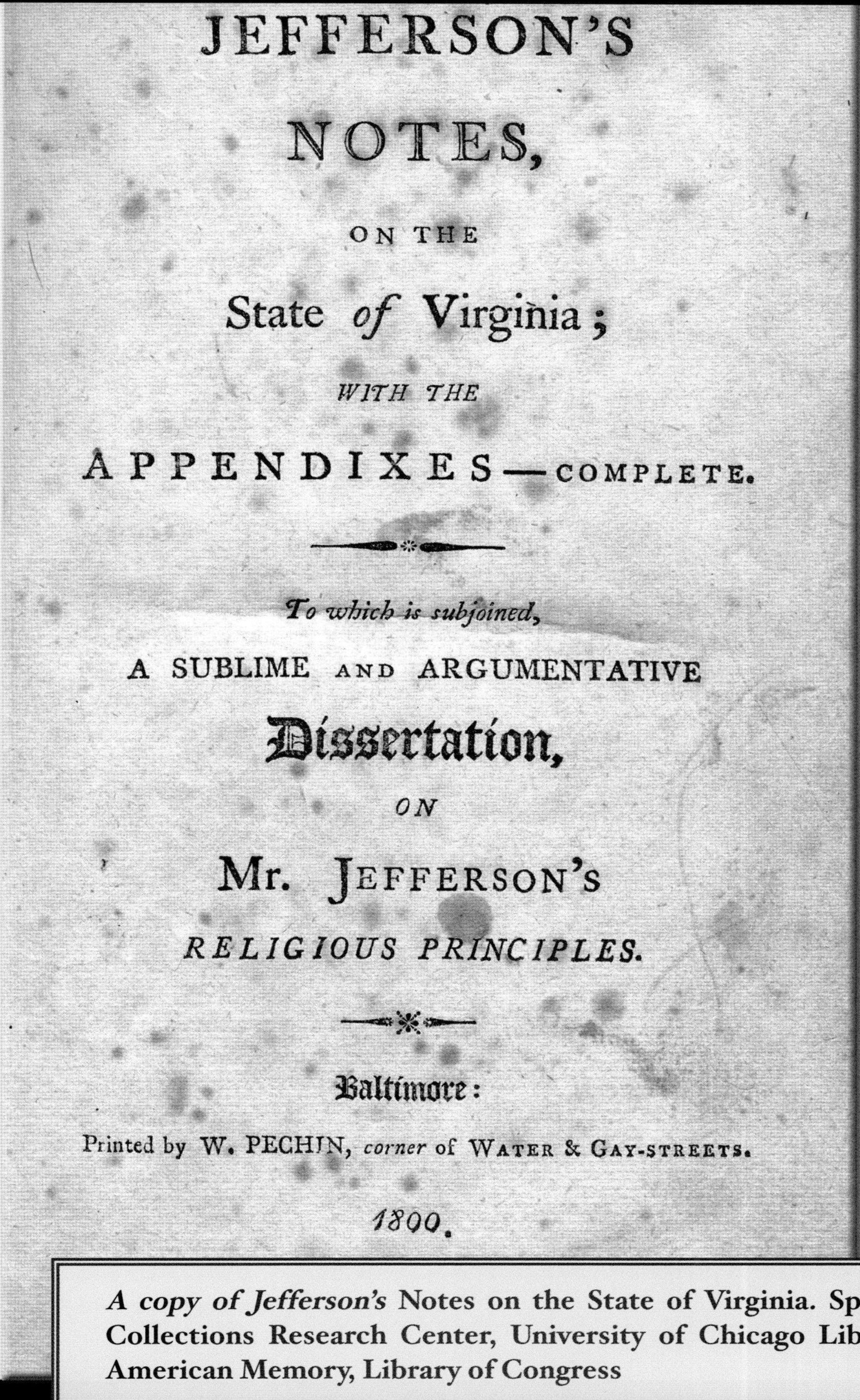

JEFFERSON'S

NOTES,

ON THE

State *of* Virginia;

WITH THE

APPENDIXES—COMPLETE.

To which is subjoined,

A SUBLIME AND ARGUMENTATIVE

Dissertation,

ON

Mr. JEFFERSON'S

RELIGIOUS PRINCIPLES.

Baltimore:

Printed by W. PECHIN, *corner* of WATER & GAY-STREETS.

1800.

A copy of Jefferson's Notes on the State of Virginia. Special Collections Research Center, University of Chicago Library. American Memory, Library of Congress

biologically inferior to whites. He believed that blacks and whites could never coexist peacefully, therefore making the ending of slavery inconceivable. Jefferson's dependence on slave labor at Monticello gave his critics another reason to describe his antislavery rhetoric as hypocritical.

CHAPTER 3

Party Politics

Jefferson returned to the United States in 1789 to serve as secretary of state under George Washington, the first president of the United States. Because the U.S. Constitution had been written and ratified while Jefferson was in Paris, he had missed the opportunity to participate in shaping the document. He criticized the framers of the Constitution for leaving out a bill of rights, arguing that every U.S. citizen was entitled to rights provided by the national government. Concerning states' rights, he contested that the authority of the federal government under the Constitution severely imposed on individual state affairs. These positions would define Jefferson's leadership role as the nation's first political parties took shape.

President George Washington (right) ***meeting with his treasury secretary, Alexander Hamilton*** (standing), ***and secretary of state, Jefferson.*** MPI/Archive Photos/Getty Images

SECRETARY OF STATE

During his tenure as secretary of state, Jefferson's principal responsibility was foreign policy. When the Napoleonic Wars between France and Great Britain began in 1793, Washington issued the Proclamation

John Adams. The Bridgeman Art Library/Getty Images

of Neutrality. However, Jefferson sought to uphold the U.S. alliance with France that was made in 1778 during the American Revolution. His political opponents, Vice President John Adams and Treasury Secretary Alexander Hamilton, favored a pro-British version of neutrality. Because of their political differences, the friendship between Jefferson and Adams that developed during their work in Paris had become jeopardized.

The U.S. government was divided between two political parties that emerged during Washington's administration: the Federalists and the Republicans. The Federalist party originated under the direction of Adams and Hamilton and promoted a strong central government. Jefferson and his political ally, James Madison, created the Republican party, which favored more autonomy within the state governments. The Republicans equated the Federalist plan of government to that of a monarchy and referred to pro-British policies as a betrayal of U.S. relations with France. Frustrated by the Federalist-controlled administration, Jefferson retired from the secretary of state office in 1793 and returned to Monticello.

Origins of the Republican Party

During George Washington's presidency, many former Anti-Federalists—who had resisted adoption of the new federal Constitution in 1787—began to unite in opposition to the economic program of Treasury Secretary Alexander Hamilton. In 1791 Hamilton and other supporters of a strong central government and a loose interpretation of the Constitution formed the

A mob storms the Bastille, a state prison in Paris, France, in 1789, at the start of the French Revolution. The fall of the Bastile came to symbolize the struggle against tyranny at the heart of the Revolution, an ideal shared by Jefferson and the Republican party. **DEA/G. Dagli Orti/De Agostini/Getty Images**

Federalist party. In response, those who favored states' rights and a strict interpretation of the Constitution rallied under Thomas Jefferson's leadership to form their own party.

Jefferson's supporters, deeply influenced by the ideals of the French Revolution (1789), first adopted the name Republican to emphasize their opposition to monarchy. The Republicans argued that the Federalists were aristocratic and that their policies placed too much power in the central government and benefited the wealthy at the expense of the common people. Although the Federalists soon branded Jefferson's followers "Democratic-Republicans," attempting to link them with the excesses of the French Revolution, the Republicans officially adopted the label in 1798. During the presidency of Andrew Jackson (1829–37), they dropped the Republican label and called themselves simply Democrats or Jacksonian Democrats. In 1844 they formally adopted the name Democratic party, which is still used today.

VICE PRESIDENT

Jefferson reentered national politics with a more stable Republican party supporting him in the presidential election of 1796. Jefferson was defeated by his political nemesis, John Adams, in a closely contested race (71 electoral votes to 68). Jefferson was made vice president because he had the second largest number of votes, in accordance with what was written in the U.S. Constitution regarding presidential elections. Jefferson occupied his years as vice president in the Senate opposing Federalist legislative actions directed by Hamilton.

In 1798 President Adams passed the Alien and Sedition Acts, which implemented tough standards for naturalization in the United States and incriminated U.S. citizens who printed antigovernment slander. Jefferson and Madison responded with the Virginia and Kentucky Resolutions of 1798–99, which protested that these acts were unconstitutional because they violated the freedom of speech clause in the First Amendment to the Constitution. As dissension between the Federalists and Republicans intensified throughout Adams' administration, Jefferson prepared for another presidential nomination.

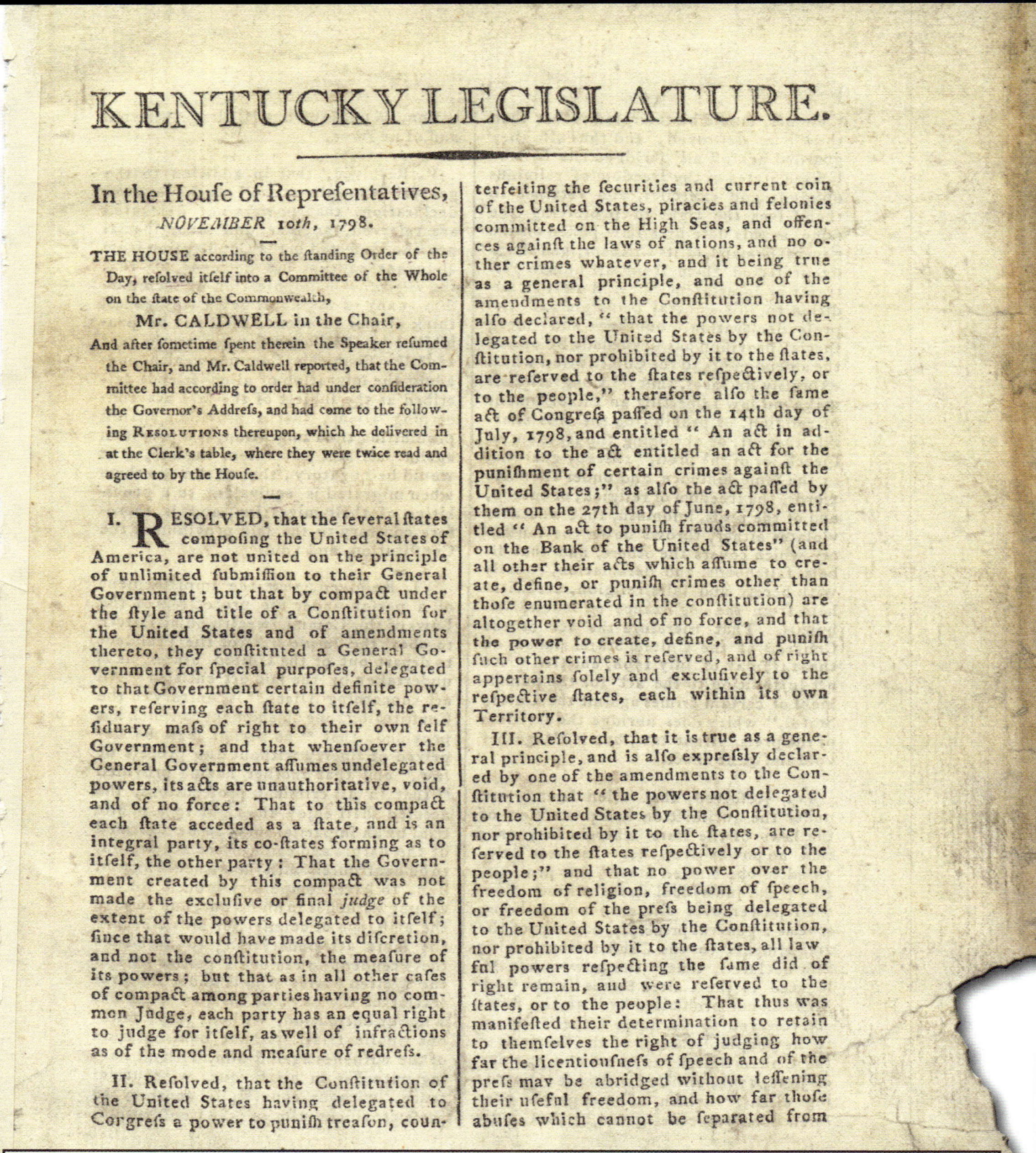

KENTUCKY LEGISLATURE.

In the Houſe of Repreſentatives,

NOVEMBER 10th, 1798.

THE HOUSE according to the ſtanding Order of the Day, reſolved itſelf into a Committee of the Whole on the ſtate of the Commonwealth,

Mr. CALDWELL in the Chair,

And after ſometime ſpent therein the Speaker reſumed the Chair, and Mr. Caldwell reported, that the Committee had according to order had under conſideration the Governor's Addreſs, and had come to the following RESOLUTIONS thereupon, which he delivered in at the Clerk's table, where they were twice read and agreed to by the Houſe.

I. RESOLVED, that the ſeveral ſtates compoſing the United States of America, are not united on the principle of unlimited ſubmiſſion to their General Government; but that by compact under the ſtyle and title of a Conſtitution for the United States and of amendments thereto, they conſtituted a General Government for ſpecial purpoſes, delegated to that Government certain definite powers, reſerving each ſtate to itſelf, the reſiduary maſs of right to their own ſelf Government; and that whenſoever the General Government aſſumes undelegated powers, its acts are unauthoritative, void, and of no force: That to this compact each ſtate acceded as a ſtate, and is an integral party, its co-ſtates forming as to itſelf, the other party: That the Government created by this compact was not made the excluſive or final *judge* of the extent of the powers delegated to itſelf; ſince that would have made its diſcretion, and not the conſtitution, the meaſure of its powers; but that as in all other caſes of compact among parties having no common Judge, each party has an equal right to judge for itſelf, as well of infractions as of the mode and meaſure of redreſs.

II. Reſolved, that the Conſtitution of the United States having delegated to Congreſs a power to puniſh treaſon, counterfeiting the ſecurities and current coin of the United States, piracies and felonies committed on the High Seas, and offences againſt the laws of nations, and no other crimes whatever, and it being true as a general principle, and one of the amendments to the Conſtitution having alſo declared, "that the powers not delegated to the United States by the Conſtitution, nor prohibited by it to the ſtates, are reſerved to the ſtates reſpectively, or to the people," therefore alſo the ſame act of Congreſs paſſed on the 14th day of July, 1798, and entitled "An act in addition to the act entitled an act for the puniſhment of certain crimes againſt the United States;" as alſo the act paſſed by them on the 27th day of June, 1798, entitled "An act to puniſh frauds committed on the Bank of the United States" (and all other their acts which aſſume to create, define, or puniſh crimes other than thoſe enumerated in the conſtitution) are altogether void and of no force, and that the power to create, define, and puniſh ſuch other crimes is reſerved, and of right appertains ſolely and excluſively to the reſpective ſtates, each within its own Territory.

III. Reſolved, that it is true as a general principle, and is alſo expreſsly declared by one of the amendments to the Conſtitution that "the powers not delegated to the United States by the Conſtitution, nor prohibited by it to the ſtates, are reſerved to the ſtates reſpectively or to the people;" and that no power over the freedom of religion, freedom of ſpeech, or freedom of the preſs being delegated to the United States by the Conſtitution, nor prohibited by it to the ſtates, all lawful powers reſpecting the ſame did of right remain, and were reſerved to the ſtates, or to the people: That thus was manifeſted their determination to retain to themſelves the right of judging how far the licentiouſneſs of ſpeech and of the preſs may be abridged without leſſening their uſeful freedom, and how far thoſe abuſes which cannot be ſeparated from

A copy of the Kentucky Resolutions. **Reuben T. Durrett Collection on Kentucky and the Ohio River Valley, Miscellaneous Manuscripts, Special Collections Research Center, University of Chicago Library. American Memory, Library of Congress**

CHAPTER 4

Presidency

In the presidential election of 1800, Jefferson squared off against Adams in another competitive campaign between the Republicans and the Federalists. Two Republicans, Jefferson and Aaron Burr of New York, tied for victory with 73 electoral votes apiece, and Adams finished with 65 electoral votes

The U.S. Constitution prevented electors from distinguishing between their choice of president and vice president on a political party's ballot. Although the voters preferred Jefferson, Burr refused to relinquish the presidency to him. Therefore, the House of Representatives convened to review the votes and decided upon Jefferson for president and Burr for vice president. To avoid a

Aaron Burr. MPI/Archive Photos/Getty Images

same-party tie in the future, the 12th Amendment to the Constitution was adopted in 1804 and required electors to cast separate ballots for president and vice president.

Jefferson was inaugurated into office on March 4, 1801. During his administration, he reduced the authority of the U.S. government by dismantling the military, lowering taxes, and decreasing the national debt. In his attempt to minimize the exposure of the presidential office, Jefferson delegated all executive messages in writing rather than through public speeches.

Jefferson's Cabinet included James Madison as secretary of state and Albert Gallatin of Pennsylvania, who was one of the nation's most qualified financial managers, as secretary of the treasury. When war between

Albert Gallatin. **Universal Images Group/Getty Images**

Great Britain and France settled temporarily in 1801, Gallatin took advantage of trade opportunities with these two countries to strengthen the U.S. economy.

TRIPOLITAN WAR

Jefferson faced his first foreign challenge from the North African Barbary state of Tripoli (now the capital of Libya). The Barbary states of Algiers, Tunis, Morocco, and Tripoli required annual tribute from U.S. vessels traveling in the Mediterranean Sea in exchange for immunity from attacks. When Tripoli increased its monetary demands, Jefferson refused to make any additional payments. Consequently, Tripoli declared war on the United States in May 1801, and Jefferson deployed U.S. warships to the North African coast.

The United States and Tripoli engaged in a naval war for the next four years. In 1804 Tripolitan forces captured the U.S. frigate *Philadelphia*, and a U.S. naval lieutenant named Stephen Decatur led a valiant raid against the overtaken frigate and destroyed it.

The combination of a U.S. naval blockade on Tripoli's coast and a U.S. land offensive

U.S. naval ships attacking the harbor of Tripoli in 1804, during the Tripolitan War. **MPI/Archive Photos/Getty Images**

into Tripoli from Egypt in the east finally ended the war. A peace treaty between the United States and Tripoli was signed on June 4, 1805, abolishing all annual tribute from the United States.

U.S. TERRITORIAL GAINS AND EXPLORATION

The Mississippi River was a valuable waterway to the western territories for the U.S. settlers who relied on the river for commerce. When Jefferson and Secretary of State Madison learned that Spain had ceded the

A map outlining the territory acquired by the United States in the Louisiana Purchase. **MPI/Archive Photos/Getty Images**

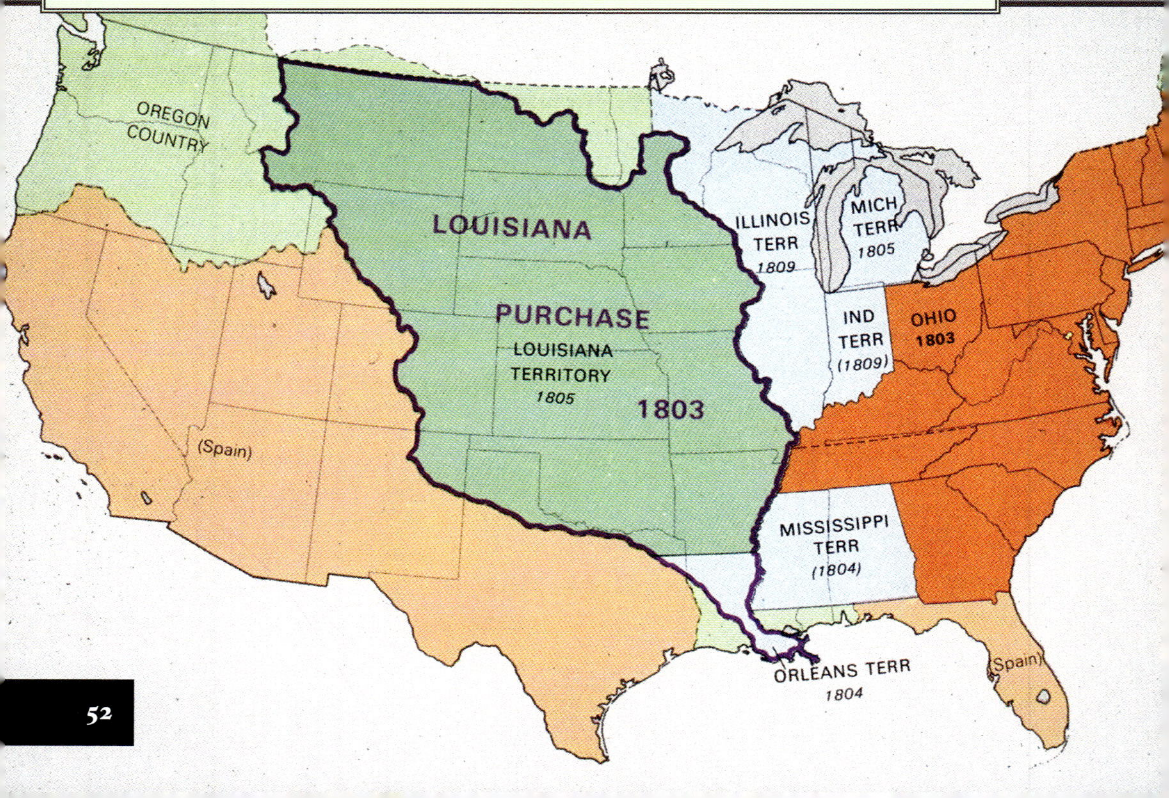

Louisiana Territory to France in the Treaty of San Ildefonso in October 1800, the U.S. leaders worried about losing access to the vital trade port at New Orleans.

Jefferson instructed U.S. ambassador to France, Robert R. Livingston, to negotiate

The Controversial Louisiana Purchase

At one stroke, the Louisiana Purchase doubled the area of the United States. President Jefferson believed that the annexation and government of so vast a territory was unconstitutional. He wanted an amendment to the Constitution to ratify it. The members of his Cabinet did not think this necessary, and their views prevailed. The New England Federalists were enraged at the prospect of the admission of numerous new states whose votes in the Senate and the House would reinforce those of the South and West. Some, such as Josiah Quincy, advocated seceding—"amicably, if they can; violently if they must." However, after due consideration and considerable debate, the Senate approved the treaty by a vote of 24 to 7.

Thirteen states, either in whole or in part, were carved out of this land between the Mississippi River and the Rockies. The price of the Louisiana Purchase was only a tiny fraction of its value today.

The expedition of Lewis and Clark. David David Gallery/ SuperStock/Getty Images

with French officials for the purchase of New Orleans. Spain also ceded West Florida to France, and Jefferson was concerned that France would restrict U.S. shipping along the entire Mississippi River. He sent James Monroe as a special envoy to assist Livingston in the negotiations with France. In a surprising turn of events, Napoleon I offered to sell the entire Louisiana Territory, which stretched from the land west of the Mississippi River to the Rocky Mountains, to the United States for $15 million. In May 1803 U.S. delegates signed a treaty with Napoleon I for the Louisiana Purchase, which was Jefferson's most celebrated achievement as president. The western territories always intrigued Jefferson because he envisioned them as the future of the United States.

In July 1803 Jefferson dispatched his private secretary, Meriwether Lewis, to lead an expedition into the newly acquired Louisiana Territory and find a passage to the Pacific

Ocean. Lewis recruited his friend, William Clark, to share command of the expedition.

Lewis and Clark's exploration party departed St. Louis, Mo., in May 1804 and headed up the Missouri River. They proceeded west, crossed the Rocky Mountains, and reached the Pacific in November 1805. Along their journey they charted maps, established friendly relations with several Native American tribes, and studied plant and animal life.

Lewis and Clark returned to St. Louis in September 1806 with detailed journals and maps and various plant and animal specimens for research. Their trail to the Pacific paved the way for future explorers and traders who sought to colonize the West.

Domestic and Foreign Challenges

Jefferson coasted to an easy victory in the presidential election of 1804 against the Federalist candidate, Charles Cotesworth Pinckney of South Carolina. Pinckney was a foreign diplomat during John Adams' administration. The influence of the Republican party under Jefferson's direction was overwhelming to the

George Clinton. MPI/Archive Photos/Getty Images

Federalists, who were unable to mount a challenging campaign. George Clinton, a former governor of New York, replaced Aaron Burr as Jefferson's vice president.

In May 1807 Burr was arrested and sent to Richmond, Va., to stand trial for treason, where Jefferson would testify against him. Burr was accused of planning an invasion into parts of the Louisiana Territory and the Spanish territories farther west. His alleged plan was to form a secessionist movement to establish a new nation under his leadership. He was acquitted of these charges in September 1807, but thereafter he lost his credibility as a political leader.

When the Napoleonic Wars resumed between Great Britain and France in 1803, Jefferson insisted that the United States uphold the Proclamation of Neutrality issued by President Washington in 1793. However, both European nations distrusted U.S. loyalties. British and French naval ships,

British naval ships destroying a French fleet in the Battle of the Basque Roads in 1809, during the Napoleonic Wars. Although the United States had remained neutral in the conflict, U.S. ships were seized by both the British and French, which led to Jefferson's signing of the Embargo Act. The Bridgeman Art Library/Getty Images

both protecting their own interests, seized U.S. merchant vessels that were suspected of carrying war supplies.

In response to the harassment at sea by Great Britain and France, Jefferson signed the Embargo Act in 1807 that closed all U.S. ports to import and export shipping. Jefferson theorized that restricting trade with the United States would convince Great Britain and France to honor U.S. neutrality.

Despite Jefferson's intentions, the Embargo Act backfired on the U.S. economy because both European countries had existing supplies of U.S. commodities. U.S. agricultural and industrial markets suffered because these businesses relied upon the income from exporting their goods. As a result of this act the United States sustained high unemployment rates.

Moreover, Jefferson's enforcement of the Embargo Act was a deviation from his opposition to coercive measures imposed by the federal government. Shortly before his term expired in 1809, Jefferson signed the Non-Intercourse Act, which allowed the United States to trade with any nation other than Great Britain and France.

Chapter 5

Retirement

Jefferson returned to Monticello in March 1809 after James Madison was inaugurated as the fourth president of the United States. Jefferson maintained an active retirement for the last 17 years of his life. He rose with the dawn each day, bathed his feet in cold water, then spent the morning on his correspondence (one year he counted writing 1,268 letters) and working in his garden. Each afternoon he took a two-hour ride around his grounds. Dinner, served in the late afternoon, was usually an occasion to gather his daughter Patsy and her 12 children, along with visitors. Monticello became a veritable hotel during these years, on occasion housing 50 guests.

Architectural Projects

Three architectural projects claimed a considerable share of Jefferson's attention. Throughout his life Monticello remained a work-in-progress that had the appearance of

Poplar Forest, the home designed by Jefferson and used as his retreat, located near Lynchburg, Va. **© Robert Harding Picture Library/SuperStock**

a construction site. Even during his retirement years, Jefferson's intensive efforts at completing the renovations never quite produced the masterpiece of neoclassical design he wanted to achieve and that modern-day visitors to Monticello find so attractive.

The lack of privacy at Monticello caused Jefferson to build a separate house on his Bedford estate about 90 miles (140 kilometers) away, which he used as a retreat. This smaller but more architecturally distinctive mansion, called Poplar Forest, was completed on schedule. It too embodied neoclassical principles but was shaped as a perfect octagon.

Finally there was the campus of the University of Virginia at Charlottesville, which Jefferson called his "academical village." Jefferson surveyed the site, which he could view in the distance from his mountaintop. He chose the Pantheon of Rome as the model for the rotunda, the centerpiece flanked by two rows of living quarters for students and faculty. In 1976 the American Institute of Architects voted it "the proudest achievement of American architecture in the past 200 years." Even the "interior" design of the University of Virginia embodied

Jefferson's principles, in that he selected all the books for the library, defined the curriculum, picked the faculty, and chaired the Board of Visitors. Unlike every other American college at the time, "Mr. Jefferson's university" had no religious affiliation and imposed no religious requirement on its students. There were no course requirements, no mandatory code of conduct except the honor system, no president or administration. Every aspect of life at the University of Virginia reflected

A statue of Jefferson stands in front of the rotunda he designed on the University of Virginia campus. **© iStockphoto.com/Bill Manning**

Jefferson's belief that the only legitimate form of governance was self-governance.

Correspondence with John Adams

In 1812 Jefferson's vast correspondence began to include an exchange with his former friend and more recent rival John Adams. The reconciliation between the two men was arranged by their mutual friend Benjamin Rush, another American patriot, who described them as "the North and South poles of the American Revolution." That description suggested how Adams and Jefferson embodied the two sides of the revolutionary generation. Jefferson represented the American Revolution as a clean break with the past, the rejection of all European versions of governing. In contrast, Adams attributed the success of the Revolution to its links with past practices, especially the tradition of representative government established in the colonial assemblies.

These genuine differences of opinion made Adams and Jefferson the odd couple of the American Revolution and were the main reasons why they had drifted to different

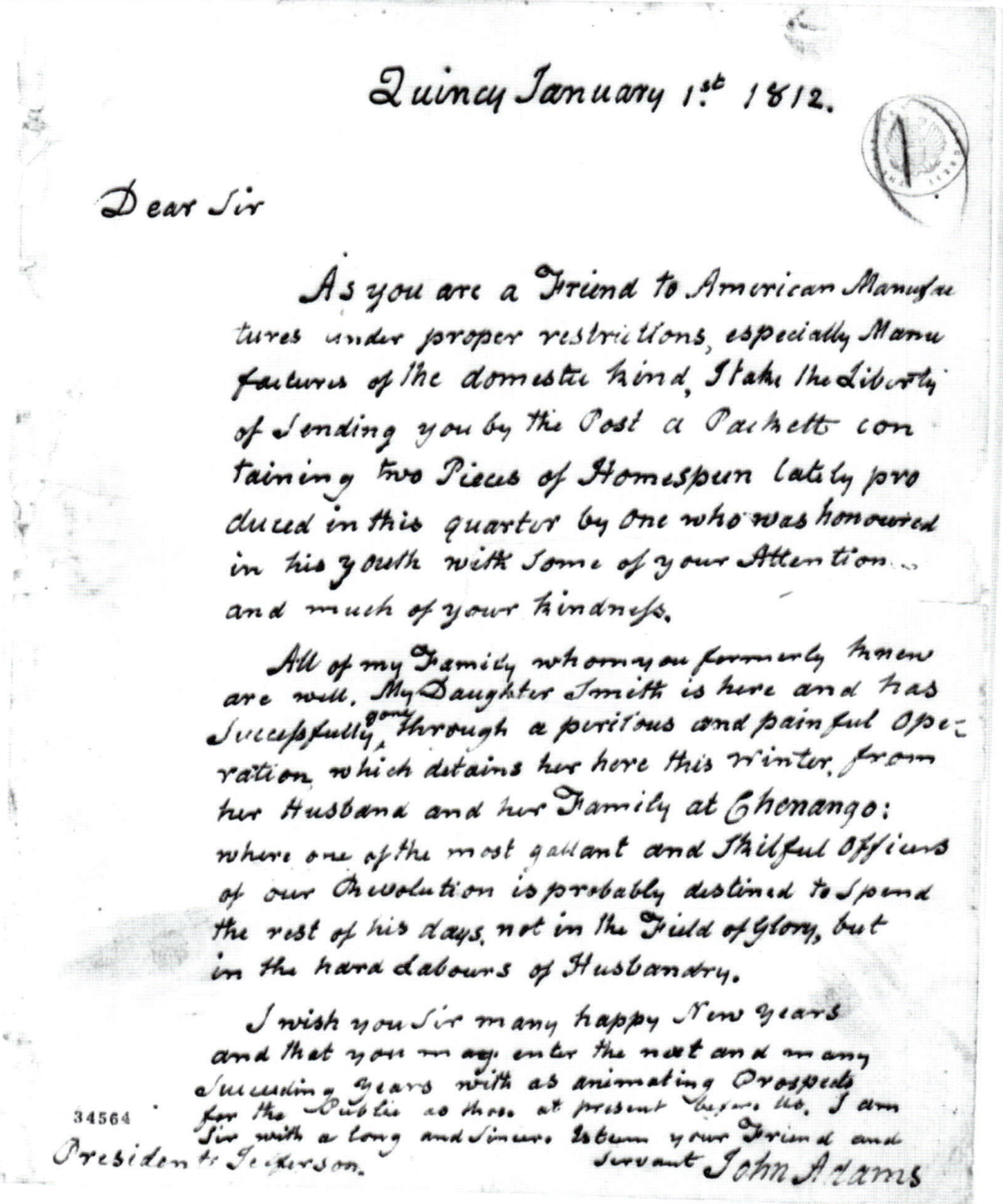

Quincy January 1st 1812.

Dear Sir

As you are a Friend to American Manufactures under proper restrictions, especially Manufactures of the domestic kind, I take the Liberty of Sending you by the Post a Packett containing two Pieces of Homespun lately produced in this quarter by One who was honoured in his youth with Some of your Attention and much of your kindness.

All of my Family whom you formerly knew are well. My Daughter Smith is here and has Successfully gone through a perilous and painful Operation, which detains her here this Winter, from her Husband and her Family at Chenango: where one of the most gallant and Skilful Officers of our Revolution is probably destined to Spend the rest of his days, not in the Field of Glory, but in the hard Labours of Husbandry.

I wish you Sir many happy New years and that you may enter the next and many Succeeding Years with as animating Prospects for the Public as those at present before Us. I am Sir with a long and Sincere Esteem your Friend and Servant John Adams

34564

President Jefferson.

A letter to Jefferson from John Adams. The Thomas Jefferson Papers. Manuscript Division, Library of Congress

Jefferson's Struggle with Debt

Apart from his stance on slavery, the other shadow that darkened Monticello during Jefferson's final years was debt. Jefferson was in debt throughout most of his life, mostly because of his lavish lifestyle. By the 1820s the interest on his debt was compounding at a faster rate than any repayment schedule could meet. By the end, he was more than $100,000—in modern terms several million dollars—in debt.

An exception was made in Virginia law to permit a lottery that Jefferson hoped would allow his heirs to keep at least a portion of his property. But the massiveness of his debt overwhelmed all such hopes. Monticello, including land, mansion, furnishings, and the vast bulk of the slave population, was auctioned off the year after his death. His surviving daughter, Patsy, was forced to accept charitable contributions to sustain her family.

sides of the divide during the party wars of the 1790s. However, the two former presidents made amends and renewed their friendship in 1812. Over the next 14 years they exchanged 158 letters in which they related personal opinions and attitudes on topics such as politics, philosophy, and religion. Their letters became the most famous correspondence between two U.S. statesmen.

The Ongoing Slavery Debate

One issue that even Adams and Jefferson could not discuss candidly was slavery. Jefferson's later position on that forbidden subject represented a further retreat from any leadership role in ending the practice. In 1819, during the debate in Congress over the Missouri Compromise, he endorsed the expansion of slavery into all the western territories, the opposite of the position he had taken in the 1780s. Furthermore, he strongly insisted that it was wrong for the federal government to attempt any effort at emancipation. His letters to fellow Virginians during his last years reflect a clear preference for secession if the U.S. government threatened any mandatory plan for abolishing slavery.

Death

On the 50th anniversary of the Declaration of Independence, July 4, 1826, Jefferson died at Monticello. He was buried in his family's

Jefferson's grave at Monticello. © iStockphotocom/Gene Krebs

cemetery on the grounds of the estate. In a symbolic coincidence in U.S. history, John Adams died within hours of Jefferson. These two legendary U.S. leaders exemplified the preservation of liberty and democracy under which the country was established.

Conclusion

Although Jefferson's reputation is surrounded by controversy over his stance on slavery and his love affairs, his efforts to preserve the welfare of his country were noble and genuine, and his achievements were numerous. The Jefferson Memorial in Washington, D.C., was completed on April 13, 1943. In the Black Hills of southwestern South Dakota, Jefferson, representing the nation's political philosophy, is one of four U.S. presidents immortalized in the colossal sculpture carved into Mount Rushmore. Both monuments honor him as one of the nation's most accomplished founders.

Glossary

Articles of Confederation First U.S. constitution (1781–89), which served as a bridge between the initial government by the Continental Congress of the Revolutionary period and the federal government provided under the U.S. Constitution of 1787.

compound interest Interest paid or to be paid both on the principal and on accumulated unpaid interest.

confederation An act of uniting persons, states, or nations into a single body.

Continental Congress In the period of the American Revolution, the body of delegates who spoke and acted collectively for the people of the colony-states that later became the United States of America. The term most specifically refers to the bodies that met in 1774 and

1775–81 and respectively designated as the First Continental Congress and the Second Continental Congress.

dissension Disagreement, especially partisan and contentious quarreling.

embargo An order of a government prohibiting the departure of commercial ships from its ports.

Federalist A member of a major political party in the early years of the United States favoring a strong centralized national government.

frigate A medium-sized square-rigged warship.

House of Burgesses Representative assembly in colonial Virginia.

incriminate To charge with or show evidence or proof of involvement in a crime or fault.

interest A charge for borrowed money, generally a percentage of the amount borrowed.

neutrality Refusal to take part in a war between other powers.

primogeniture An exclusive right of inheritance belonging to the eldest son.

Republican A member of a major political party in the early years of the

United States favoring a smaller central government, states' rights, and strict interpretation of the U.S. Constitution.

rhetoric Verbal communication; discourse.

secede To withdraw from an organization.

sedition The offense of organizing or encouraging opposition to government.

slander The expression of false charges or misrepresentations that defame and damage another's reputation.

statutory Enacted, created, or regulated by statute, or law.

treason The crime of betraying a nation or a sovereign by acts considered dangerous to security.

For More Information

American Historical Association (AHA)
400 A Street SE
Washington, DC 20003
(202) 544-2422
Web site: http://www.historians.org
The AHA serves as a leader and advocate for professionals, researchers, and students in the field of history and upholds academic and professional standards. The AHA also awards a number of fellowships and prizes and offers resources and publications for anyone interested in the field.

Miller Center
2201 Old Ivy Road
Charlottesville, VA 22904
(434) 924-7236
Web site: http://millercenter.org

The Miller Center at the University of Virginia furthers understanding of the presidency, political history, and policy through its various research initiatives, programs, events, and fellowship opportunities.

Monticello
Thomas Jefferson Foundation
P.O. Box 316
Charlottesville, VA 22902
(434) 984-9822
Web site: http://www.monticello.org
Visitors to Monticello can tour Thomas Jefferson's historic home, grounds, and plantation and learn about his life through films, exhibits, and activities.

National Museum of American History (NMAH)
1400 Constitution Avenue NW
Washington, DC 20560
(202) 633-1000
Web site: http://americanhistory.si.edu
With more than 3 million artifacts of American history in its collection, many of which are on display, the NMAH is dedicated to promoting public interest

in the events that shaped the American nation. Its *The American Presidency: A Glorious Burden* exhibit profiles American presidents through collections of their personal belongings , campaign memorabilia, and many other items.

Poplar Forest
1542 Bateman Bridge Road
Forest, VA 24551
(434) 525-1806
Web site: http://www.poplarforest.org
Designed by Thomas Jefferson and used as his personal retreat, Poplar Forest is now open to the public for tours. Programs and resources related to architecture, archaeology, and more are also offered.

Web Sites

Due to the changing nature of Internet links, Rosen Educational Services has developed an online list of Web sites related to the subject of this book. This site is updated regularly. Please use this link to access the list:

http://www.rosenlinks.com/pppl/thomj

For Further Reading

Ambrose, S.E. *Undaunted Courage* (Simon & Schuster, 1996).

Bernstein, R.B. *Thomas Jefferson: The Revolution of Ideas* (Oxford Univ. Press, 2004).

Bober, Natalie. *Thomas Jefferson: Draftsman of a Nation* (Univ. Of Virginia Press, 2008).

Commager, H.S. *Jefferson, Nationalism, and the Enlightenment* (Braziller, 1986).

Cunningham, N.E., Jr. *Jefferson vs. Hamilton: Confrontations That Shaped a Nation* (Bedford/St. Martin's, 2000).

Ford, P.L., ed. *The Autobiography of Thomas Jefferson, 1743–1790* (Univ. of Pennsylvania Press, 2005; orig. pub. 1914).

Lanier, Shannon. *Jefferson's Children: The Story of One American Family* (Random House, 2002).

Malone, Dumas. *Jefferson and His Time,* 6 vols. (Univ. of Virginia Press, 2005).

McLaughlin, Jack. *Jefferson and Monticello: The Biography of a Builder* (Holt, 1990).

Meltzer, Milton. *Thomas Jefferson: The Revolutionary Aristocrat* (Franklin Watts, 1991).

Whitelaw, Nancy. *Thomas Jefferson: Philosopher and President* (Morgan Reynolds, 2002)

Index